# The Music

## New and Selected Poems
## 1973-2023

## Everett Hoagland

**WILLOW BOOKS**
Detroit, Michigan

**The Music:**
**New and Selected Poems, 1973-2023**

ISBN  979-8-9881655-3-8

Cover photo:  Musician Benjamin Richard Hoagland, Everett Hoagland's great-grandfather

Cover design: Aquarius Press LLC

Willow Books, a Division of Aquarius Press
www.WillowLit.net

Printed in the United States of America

*For Kita, Kamal, Nia, Ayan, and Reza*

# Contents

# THE MUSIC

# COMMUNION

# WORD!

# JAZZ THEOLOGY

ACKNOWLEDGEMENTS

Thanks to the editors of the following periodicals in which these poems, some in different versions, previously appeared:

*The American Poetry Review*: "Communion" (as "Cookin'"), "Keeping The Faith," "Kinda Blue: Miles Davis Died Today," "Red, White, and Blues Country," "Undoing The 'Do," "Bob Kaufman?"

*Callaloo*: "Walking Kaufman Home"

*The Unitarian Universalist World Magazine*: "Nia," "Umoja," "Homecoming," "As I Ebb Toward the End of Life"

Thanks also to the editors of the following publications in which these poems, some in different versions, previously appeared:

"In The Boston MFA," *The Progressive* and *Black Renaissance*; New York, Fall 2009/Winter 2010.

"All That: Fred Ho" appeared in *Afro Asia: Revolutionary Political & Cultural Connections Between African Americans & Asian Americans*, edited by Fred Ho and Bill V. Mullen, published by Duke University Press, 2008.

"Homecoming" also appeared in *African American Literature*, edited by Keith Gilyard and Anissa Wardi, published by Penguin Academics/Pearson-Longman, 2004.

"Everett/Imamu/Amiri" (as the longer version of "you should be shoo be") appeared in *The Best American Poetry 2002*, edited by Robert Creeley and David Lehman, published by Scribner, 2002.

"Love Jam" appeared in *bum rush the page: a def poetry jam*, edited by Tony Medina and Lous Reyes Rivera, published by Three Rivers Press, 2001.

"Love Jam" (as "Jamming") and "The Music" (as published in the first edition of this book) appeared in *The Jazz Poetry Anthology*, edited by Sascha Feinstein and Yusef Komunyakaa, published by Indiana University Press, 1991.

"Amiri's Next Set" appeared in *Tambou*, an online zine, 2014.

"The Music" (as it appears in this volume) was originally published as "FOR B.R.E.A.T.H.E." *THE WAYS: Poems of Affirmation, Remembrance, Reflection, and Wonder*, North Star Nova Press, 2022.

"The Music" appeared in *Bluu Notes*, edited by Takiyah Nur Amin and Mykal Slack, 2022.

"Sister Say" and "A Big B.A.M. Theory of Creation" appeared in *Black Fire This Time*, edited by Kim Mcmillon, published by Willow Books, a Division of Aquarius Press, 2022

"The Music" (as "For B.R.E.A.T.H.E.") and "…To You." appeared in *The Social Protests of 2020: Police Brutality, Covid 19 and Circumscribed Sexuality*, edited by Joyce Ann Joyce, 2023.

Also, thanks to Tracey Saloman for typing the updated manuscript and for all her astute technical advice.

# INTRODUCTION

*"Poems are rough notations for the music we are."* — Rumi

Why a second edition of my 2014 - 2015 book, *THE MUSIC and Other Selected Poems*? Why not? So much has happened since then, much of which inspired my recent poetry: the rise of mass, open-ly fascist Right-Wing politics (a kind of third post-Reconstruction), Covid, accountability-facilitating video-taped murders of black people by police, revitalization of Black Lives Matter types of orga-nized mass protest, etc.

Many watched on TV as "January 6th" happened at the Capitol Building in Washington, DC, and saw a seditious riot, an attempt to effect a treasonous takeover of the national government. Poets look at something and see more than what is there; we also see what that something suggests. So watching January 6th I saw what hap-pened at/to Black Tulsa, Rosewood and the MANY other murder-ous takeovers and destructions of African American communities in this country's history as are noted on the Equal Justice Institute's righteous annual curriculum-like calendars, lest we forget. Because the fact is, one way or another, Amerikkka still *happens* to African Americans every day.

Fully conscious vocal artist, superb pianist and lyricist, Nina Sim-one, said artists, including poets, should *"Reflect the times."* Tradi-tionally, among many other things, African American poets have been/are testamentary. And conscious African American poets have never been reluctant to "rock the boat," rock the 1619 slave ship still moored in Amerikkka's history. Because we know we are still bobbing on the ripples emanating from it, and still treading water in those ripples.

Four centuries of political ripples, social ripples, economic ripples, psychological ripples. Yet sublime and life-loving, liberty-loving, pursuit-of-happiness-loving artistic expression of hope and faith have risen, and still rise from under and on the surface of the trou-bled waters on which that slave ship's three-thousand-mile wake can still be sensed. If you know how to read water as poets have and do. Know how to read tears, blood and sweat, as well as being able to read Cape Fear River the way Sweet Honey In The Rock did, and if you are able to read Amerikkka's pulsing aorta, the storied

11

Mississippi. Indeed, as Langston Hughes wrote, "we *have* known rivers..."

Yet ancestral and contemporary, testamentary, artistic reactions to all that victimization, inhumanity and ugliness rise truth-tellingly, beautifully, in The Music reminding us how we can remember the future, just as we always have, as urged in the first and second verses of the poem-turned-into-song, "Lift Every Voice and Sing"; and Nina Simone's defiantly worded songs "Mississippi, God Damn!", "To Be Young, Gifted and Black"; and John Coltrane's transcendent, "A Love Supreme"; Gil Scot-Heron's "Free Will"; Rhiannon Giddens' Quartet's "Music and Joy," "You're Not Alone".

The Music. When most of the African Americans from my generation use that term, they are referring to jazz. But the poems in this collection mention spirituals, blues, jazz, gospel, R&B, world music, hip hop, even country & western. Otherwise, the poems celebrate or eulogize jazz musicians and jazz poets, or make metaphorical suggestions about a connection between jazz performance and love relationships, as well as a suggestion about a symbolic relationship among jazz band performance, life, and death. One poem ambitiously tries to combine most of these things and also tries to imitate the improvisational modality of jazz.

The poems in this collection were written and published between 1973 through 2023. This book was conceived many years ago, decades ago, and it would have been titled *The Music*. But my friend the late Amiri Baraka had recently given that title to a book of his own poetry. So, I had to improvise to keep the title's first two words in the mix.

I suspect many of us who are African American poets would really prefer to be masterful musicians. Maybe that is why so much black poetry — from Dunbar, J.W. Johnson, Langston Hughes, Sterling Brown, Margaret Walker, Maya Angelou, Jayne Cortez, Amiri Baraka, Kalamu Ya Salaam, Jessica Care Moore, and Climbing Poetree's Naima and Alixa — is so downright musical. Some like Sun Ra, Gil Scott-Heron, have actually been musicians, songified lyrical poets. We have always had them, from the Djalis to the hip hop poets. Considering all of the blanching we have been subjected to it is amazing how much ancient African culture and tradition is extant (much of it, like the music, creolized) in African American culture.

It is also amazing how many aspects of that culture have been and continue to be predominant expressions of *American* culture.

Here are two short anecdotes about my disposition re: where The Music (as jazz) comes from and where it takes me.

When Ken Burns' documentary series *JAZZ* came out, a European American music teacher told me, "Burns spent too much time on Armstrong." I told him, "That's a little like accusing someone doing a documentary on Christianity of spending too much time on Jesus!" And a friend in my spiritual community once said, "When the time comes, I'm willingly going into the light." I replied, "When the time comes for me, I hope I have on my headphones, because I want to 'go' into The Music."

—Everett Hoagland

# FOREWORD

*For B.R.E.A.T.H.E.*
*A New Bedford Social*
*Justice Collective*

*NO JUSTICE, NO PEACE!!*

This has been a spring
of cut flowers in hospital
shops' vases. A season

of virtual hugs, ghost pleasure
of what has been
cut-

off, cut-out, zapped. A time
of ZOOM screened phone
& laptop kisses, ever more

acronyms & agonized mass
hospital dyings, police killings,
without family or live last rites.

Tablets of Thou Shall Not
WHO & CDC commandments.
This Juneteeth's soundtrack is sirens,
march time chanting *NO*
*JUSTICE, NO PEACE,*
LOUD honking, warning-
giving car caravans' horns
at the intersection of yesterday,
today & tomorrow blast

the wrongful Right's
Jericho walls
all around us. Loop

the cities past
memorial murals painted
with blood, white lies &

15

indivisible video-recorded
blues while making a way
toward a perfectly pitched

modulation in a
harmonious rendition
of America, The Beautiful,

that rings
truer *HA!*
than the cracked Liberty Bell.
An old anthem,
since the indigo trade
out of Africa, that despite

The Declaration
has variously been, yes,
a slave work song, yes,

a "negro" spiritual, prison
labor song, strangely fruited
jazz tree song, Lift Every Voice,

yes, We Shall
Overcome, yes,
& righteous rage-freighted

rap. The nation
is again at the bridge
of an echoing crossroad blues.

An alternate lyric of something
chanted differently every fifty years
or so. The same old road song

riffed again
& again. But not by just *us*
now, with masses of allies chiming

in *this* time. While on the only road
forward, onward we have ever had.

Hell, yes, *NO*

*JUSTICE, NO PEACE!!* Yes,
*NO JUSTICE, NO PEACE!!!*

Peace!

Juneteenth 2020

# THE MUSIC

# PICTURE THIS

*For Police-Murdered Tyre Nickols*

Who does not like looking at striking sunsets'
satin sheens? We can all picture one from memory.

Who cannot picture amateur photographer
Tyre Nickols, looking at how fast-

changing pastel tones, how lit late days' hues
color evening air on the eastern horizon, merge, meld

near where he lived before he was beaten, kicked, stomped
to death by in-uniform thug-agents of the state of things,

who cam-motion-pictured their own crime. Picture him
marveling at the way.

variously every clear yet ending, fading day reddens blues
to purple, how dusk's pink softens purple to violet so

similarly different every day. Who cannot see how
it could make him smile as he selfied himself

in its foreground … And I find myself picturing him
in my mind the way photographers used to develop negatives

by immersion in developing fluid trays. As for the positive
young man I did not know but did and do to the degree

he was/is me, you, in his humanity, picture that.
Picture him, picture Tyre standing quietly still listening

to sunsets' silent music, the kind heard only with one's eyes.
Picture that. It will help you remember tomorrow.


2023

## "GREAT DAY IN THE MORNING!"

This morning's news broadcast was all
about the manmade bad things

happening almost everywhere.
I rose from my laptop, table, chair,

turned on recorded music, Dexter Gordon's poignant
sax, wordlessly telling us the good news

about us all. Everywhere. Which
leavens the news; it breaks us

open to one another as our spirits'
daily bread. Went back to my laptop, sat,

found myself holding that morning's
background music to an inner ear, found

myself in a mist rising from the ocean
blues-hued jazz of Yusef Komunyakaa's "African

Burial Ground"[1] where *everything* is
excavated in the mirror that faces me

each morning like silent ripples of concentric
visual rhythms, soundless drum beats & coded

Ogun icons hidden in lost-wax cast metal masks, iron fences'
gates & wordless patchwork hand-me-

down, stitched story quilts along a people's life lines
on open palm-like, cured tobacco leaves & in the weave

of soft cotton's hard historical facts. Pan-human aspects
of being, such as that ochre hand print left

on a torch lit cave wall. The urge to image,
to silently say I was, we were here, found

visualized or as aurally expressed

folk experience by sounding the depths

of group mores & memories one way
or another everywhere we have been us.


2020

## ON FREE WILL AND THE RIGHTS OF MAN

Tall Thomas Jefferson's DNA
is the real writing on the White
House wall, a semen stained graffito:

*...cry Sally cry*
*close your anxious eyes*
*turn to the north*
*turn to the south*
*turn to the one with the prettiest lies*
*in his mouth...*

Teenaged quadroon Sally Hemings may have crossed her-
self many times contemplating the slave ships'
blacks' gray sea cemetery
her forebears crossed while she criss-
crossed the old New World Middle
Passage as an African
American serving her master's daughter,
who was her niece.

In the course of human events in Paris
The Founding Father initiated a (38 year)
affair with fifteen year old, relatively
"fair" Dusky Sally who he owned, and bye
the bye, by whom he had children. But
today we are told the bright inventor
of the dumbwaiter was, after all, a man
of his time. *Things* were different then
for those of us now up from slavery and down from

Jefferson. When he nightly, tightly,
held his inherited Happiness face to face
did her handsome charms make him tremble
in her arms when he remembered the Self-

Evident truth that...*God is just*?

The Founding Father kept her, if not his blood-
stained word, and did not will her free. "Mighty near white... "
Sally Hemings did what she had to

do, day and night, survived her master's
Brotherly Love and died free. Our nation's
Liberty Tree is rooted in her grave. In mind
her headstone read:

*Free at last free…*
*If you didn't like my peaches*
*why'd you shake my tree?*

Her descendants freely finger desiccated, yellow
pages of a partly executed legacy
printed on dried peach skin peeled off Nat Turner,
reproduced en masse and for sale:
facsimile memento copies of *The Declaration.*

And right down to today
our oral histories say, not only
did one of our presidents' kids have black
blood, one of our presidents was by white Black Codes

a Blood! By the laws by the men of his time.
Idealistic, conflicted, all–
too-human Humanist Jefferson, indeed,
should have, could have, would have

found it a *degradation* that history
has pursued him like a bloodhound;
that hard science has colored the cold, white
lie with a woman's warm, soft, pliant body politic;
her Virginia Bright, tobacco leaf skin; long,
straight, dark …down her veiled, black monotony…

…back by night the brilliant Founding Father
lay with the light black childwoman
who was by white blood his sister-
in-law, but, by *The Rights of Man*
and law, his slave, and begot Madison,
Beverly, Harriet and Eston. "Vicissitudes," we are

told, "the way of the world." And we now know all
the wherefores, the whereof, the whereas
and Y. And long ago learned that

The Big House can, indeed, stand divided
against itself and unbecomingly
become The Executive Mansion,
Enlightenment University,
corporate headquarters,
and a neoclassical national shrine.

*...ride Sally ride*
*open wide your loving eyes*
*turn to the north*
*turn to the south*
*turn sternly to the one with*
*The Whitest Lies*
*in his mouth...*

1998

# From, JUST WORDS: FREDERICK DOUGLASS, 1838

*I am a poor pilgrim of sorrow…*
*Sometimes I don't know where to roam…*
*…But I've heard of a city called Heaven*
*And I've started to make it my home.*

Dead Fred Douglass alive
in the after-life of The Word:

*…no more*
*driver's lash for me, no more,*
*no more…*
*The gospel train's a-comin'*
*I hear it rumblin' through the land.*
*The poorest of poor can go,*
*with their fare in their hand;*
*the fare is faith and struggle.*
*So what we waitin' for? Get on board,*
*Children, there's room for many a-more.*

"If there is no struggle, there is no progress…"

Just words in hand, on borrowed free
merchant seaman's papers loaned
by brother Freeblood. Given
meager money and abundant love,
in Baltimore your freedom financed by fiancée,
free born Anna Murray, who
risking all, would marry you
on a side-track at a way station in New York City.

And, so, wearing her heart's handiwork,
disguised as a sailor in a blood red shirt,
tarp hat, black cravat, you boarded the train
in Maryland at Mercy Station, north
bound to Jubilee Terminal,
where you would be

free…

…FREE, at last…

in standup Brother Nathan Johnson's house,
at Mercy's Wellspring
and Seventh Heaven Streets
in New Bedford's Abolitionists' Village
on that Great Gettin' Up Mornin', where
barely there you are
re-renamed. You'd been bound
as Bailey, journeyed as Johnson
and, by Nathan's reading of a poem —

just words — at your overground, under-
ground train trip's last stop, steeped
in words, baptized in purpose you came
roaring out of Nathan and Polly Johnson's door,

reborn lean and leonine Frederick Douglass
of the life-long, reasoned, rhetorical roar:

"Power concedes nothing without a demand;
it never did and it never will."

The still reverberating roar
tells those content to quietly wait
for justice,
Don't leave life to chance or fate!

"Agitate! Agitate!! Agitate!!!"

Your roar reminds us
how we have been and should be
Fred-Douglass-alive
in the afterlife of his words:

*...I've heard of a city called Heaven*
*And I've started to make it my home.*

1995

## HAMMER MAN: LEWIS TEMPLE: 1848

…Your own bondage long
since over, by 1848 in New Bedford,
that Shining City On A Hill just south
of The North Star, where you were
blacksmithed in redundancy.

Eager to advance yourself
in an industry equally open
to seamen of
all colors and kinds

your mind was lit
by a pivotal epiphany
as if by whale oil lamp
or a temple's votive candle.

And you hammered white
hot lies bellowed by bullying
pro-slavery orators into a shaft
of black light that would hold true.
You beat them with rage as though
they were bars of some personal cage.

You added, heated slavery's scrap
ironies and hammered them
on your anvil.

Smartly
struck,
pounded,
beat them.

Hard
hammered the slaver's
branding iron chain-
links, manacles,
shackles, you
fired,
tempered in black
blood, forged, fashioned

29

Temple's Toggle, Temple's Iron

an unfailing
harpoon worthy of *Ogun.*[2]
Soon touted, toted as "the most important
invention in the whole history
of whaling,"[3] making all whales right whales
for profits from oil, bone, baleen sales.

And once upon a whale-taled time
antebellum New Bedford thereby
briefly came to be the world's
richest city by the sea, "The city that lit the world."


2007

**AFTER READING** *ALL GOD'S DANGERS: THE LIFE OF*
*NATE SHAW*[4]

Your archival voice,
our long blues song,
life's story
coughed up
the blood-soaked cotton
gag. Blue blood,
book-long,
blue steel guitar blues.

Your Smith and Wesson
.32 gun metal voice.

What did they call you
when you resisted?

*"If you were*
*a white man: principled,*
*mule: stubborn,*
*nigger: crazy."*

You were a blue steel guitar,

and your wife was
a fiddle and a tambourine,
Hannah. Soft as cotton
and as strong.
And your wife was
a fiddle and a tambourine
and we your sons are
canefifes,
we your daughters
banjos,
playing your gun metal voice,
playing your blue steel
guitar book-long song

*CRAZY!*

# THE LAST SCOTTSBORO "BOY"

You might have thought justice
was a jive, cracked tune,
sung with a forked tongue,
like the Liberty Bell's.

But you held life
like a steel guitar, your jail cell
a twelve-bar blues, and strummed it:

*All people should be free.*

In Alabama, the governor's
pardon, Wallace gives you some skin.
His representative and Miss Belle
try to ring Liberty, but
it's Alabama
and you know it's a blues tune:

*Clarence Norris, aged 63.*
*I have no hate;*
*I like all people.*
*All people should be*
*free. I wish those other boys were around to*
*see…*

1976

## THE "TO SERVE AND PROTECT" BLUES

Have you seen the obscene
photos of inhumanity?
He was killed. Just
died, they say
expertly,
of an overdose! Just

as he died over,
and over
down
in the stinking, choking hold
of the slave ship *Gracia de Dios*…Just
as he died
a million X's
over the diaspora
choking on strange, blue fruit
from The Human Family Tree.

His own folk testify with *mornas*
over sea-green-blues
of our history.

One way or another
arrested,
he died in a jail cell
in a tradition, a custom:
protective custody.
At first he was
unwilling,
then he wasn't

able to throw down,
throw up the evidence
of the swallowed crime.

The old, old ritual: Whipping Boy.
Beaten
over and over
again
with snarls, sneers, jeers.

His still color
photo, bloody,
flattened face the face
of Emmett Till beneath the still waters.
The face of Rodney King
"Kong" still in the eyes
of the perpetrator. The face
of George Floyd.

Brother, Sister, one way or another
Morris Pina's telling Rorschach bruises
his misshapen head, body
bag
are emblematic of the old cult's
id.
They give the lie to those
who
fairly say he died justly.

No. He was not
an Innocent. Neither was
he proven guilty. One way
or another
there is no life

sentence; there is no death
sentence in this state
of Massassippi
for the wrong-
full death of a "…black
son-of-a-bitch!" Or Beantown's
old, sick, retired reverend, who
was scared to death in his living room
in a wrongful drug raid.

Over and over
again, the fear of Post-Reconstruction.
The Depression and Eisenhower years.
The temper, the tone,
the times bear it out, bare
the old ritual standard:

BLACK MAN IN CUSTODY DEAD

of an Overdose of Service and Protection.

All's right with the good
Ol' U.S. of

*eh?*


1994

# LEGACIES

*"...the eyes of my father...when*
*he died, closed...opened...in me"*
— From "Glory" by Gbenga Adesina

At the end of our living
room hospice for him

twenty-four years ago,
with my right hand's thumb

and other two writing fingers,
I closed my just dead father's half-

opened eyes. Even now,
I, almost as old as he was then,

remember remembering
everything at once. Including to what

in black and white and in blue
uniforms, by his caring paternal way

he had opened mine: *The Conversation.*
That passed on, "dead up" life-

saving but joyless legacy I have
long since shared with my grandsons

more than once, while working in mention
of our culture's durable resistance-and-

struggle-ethic dream, mountain metaphor.
And sung crossroad ways by which folk,

*yes*, had incrementally come out of "no
way" up to today's marching toward

Black Lives' human rights justice
with allies. Me mixing the starkly

36

blood red, white and blued message
to and for my grandboys with:

our testamentary orature, hilarious
heirloom barbershop lore, my great-uncle

Willie's father-wit, our jubilant jazz,
jokes, jive, among the other spirited things

in our handed-down survival kit
that help to keep us alive,

life-loving, laughing, stand-
up, open, until we close,

or someone, something
else closes our eyes.


2022

# MANY THOUSANDS THOUSAND GONE

They are not just
statistics, not just numbers.
They are our grown kids and grandkids.
They are our heartbeats. Let us say their names:

Morris Pina, Trayvon Martin, Eric Garner,
Michael Brown.
Tamir Rice, Akai Gurley, Rumain Briston,
Ezel Ford,
Timothy Russell, Malissa Williams, Sandra Bland...

*BLACK LIVES MATTER!*

Hey, they kill unarmed black girls and women, too.
Hell yes, they do!

Though one would have been
too many, how many children cried
and died on the coastward trek in coffles?
How many soon died of diet, shock, or behind the dark curtain
of depression in the barracoons like Goree? How many died
of flux in the suffocating hold of the slave ship *Gracia De Dios*
during the four centuries of the African slave trade? God, how many?

*BLACK LIVES MATTER!*

How many with their last moans
flew home to Africa during the first soul-chilling snow
after auction block? How many
galloped away in the night on a white, red-speckled horse
named Consumption? How many
tiny bundled ones froze or burned up with fever in parents' arms
on The Underground Railroad?

*BLACK LIVES MATTER!*

It kills and kills. How many
Emmet Tills have we had?
If it was or is only one child,
one would be too many.

So why are so many of those uniformed in blue hues
forcing so many lethal overdoses of Service and Protection
onto those who in any clothes are uniformly blues people?
What is it in some that makes them kill our kids and grandkids
on sight, on site makes them irrationally angry
or full of fright, gives them excuse to abuse
their uncivil civic might?

*BLACK LIVES MATTER!*

What does it profit them to create this mass
incarceration state at such a rate? Well, hell, what profited
from its holdings in slave ships? What got rich off the quarters
behind Mount Vernon and Monticello and waxed fat from fields
of indigo-dyed cotton blues? And still does by nixing really righ-
teous raps'
raw anger at The State of Things?

The ugly id of Amerika kills and kills unarmed kids
with impunity, as if with some kind of diplomatic immunity. The
hate kills,
wrongfully outright murders people of color it cannot incarcerate
in this mass-prisons-for-profits state. We hold *these* truths to be
self-evident:

Morris, Trayvon, Eric, Malcolm Michael, Tamir, Akai, Rumain,
Ezel, Tony,
Timothy, Malissa, Sandra, Tyre, Breanna…

*BLACK LIVES MATTER!*

Who are the accomplices in all of this? Those of us unwilling to
fight
to change a system that profits from crack and heroin addiction,
from under-funded public schools, reversed voting rights,
The State-of-Hate's legislatures that will not enact
laws to prosecute cops for murders of unarmed
citizens, from ghettos, mass joblessness,
from mass jailings' labor camps…
and so around and around
it goes. And so go we.

See?

*BLACK LIVES MATTER!*
Though one would be too many,
how many unarmed black boys, men, girls, women
of color have been copped, objectified, commodified wrong-
fully outright killed? Many, many

*MILLIONS!!!!!!!*

Millions by the dozens, millions by the score.
Come on good people, let us make sure there are
no more, no more. Power To The People!!!

*BLACK LIVES MATTER!*
*BLACK LIVES MATTER!!*
*BLACK LIVES MATTER!!!*


2014, 2017

# "ILLEGAL" IMMIGRANTS & LEGAL INHUMANITY

after columbus came in the name of God
& the reign of spain & his crew did what
was done to tainos arawks mayans

after cortez & his mounted cortege
undid the aztecs & others of *los indios*
& recast the conquered cultures into ingots
gold altars & coins

after pious puritans became populous
& plotted to perpetrate genocide
again the connecticut pequot

who are **we the people** but a nation
of emigrated immigrants? who
are **we the people** to oppressively oversee
the exclusion of k'iche-speaking
tzeltal-speaking mam-speaking spanish-speaking
portuguese-speaking english-speaking
danish-speaking french-speaking people

of color whose central american south american
antillean & african ancestors were already in or
forcibly brought sold & bought in diverse places
in the americas long before arrivals
of europe's "huddled masses"?

who are **we the people** to keep people
from cropping the "amber waves of grain"
from making hay of the *leaves of grass*
in the promised land of our anthems
& all-american poetry

from working as rightful migrants at any
righteous endeavors to better themselves including
"in the vineyards where the grapes of wrath are stored"
or from harvesting the field from which we get
"our daily bread"????

*Lord!!!*

## ALL THAT: FRED HO

here you are
just as surely as all
arabian
barbary
spanish
horses
native american
mustangs
are of asian origin      you

are here in karmic world music
with bass clef lapels large
as plane wings          your trademark
red silk zoot suit — spun
as much from ananse's akan
trickster webs of sonic yarn
as from mandarin silk worms —

is all that      just
as surely as ancient giant
chinese merchant ships with four-square
sails big and red as sunset plied the indian

ocean  just as surely as indians traded with east

africans who traded with arabs
who traded in african slaves
in the name of   the one   the merciful   just
as surely as hulled middle passage
floating white hells with holds full
of iron-collared captives branded "black

devils" were named *mercy* & everything
between *angel* & *zong* oceanic weaves
logged cross-stitching mapped the patterned kente warp
& woof of moaned american music   just

as surely as communal rum-brown afro-
cuban hands life-lined like cured tobacco
leaves freely drum whatever ogun & shango
congas mambos sambas they damn
well please africans chinese indians mix

it up in trinidad's steel pan bands that play
paisley raindrops pinging corrugated tin
balafon rooftops on plum fluted trade
winds swishing hushes in palm trees from

beached coconuts washed up by measureless
water music refrains of singing seas'
deep sounding whales'
songs that buoyed net numbers of hopeful
chinese laborers who over-

came the choke-holds of money's
dead calm pacific migrant ships
their hands cradling stern urns of ancestors'
dust & empty heirloom blue willow ginger jars
full of silent music

whole-nine-yards of child labor magic
"oriental" rugs woven with all the over
tones under
tones of pan-people music

here you are

jacketed with the fly-away lapels of zoot-
winged victory as brass flame saxophone dragon
suits you    pressed as you want to be in your all-
american ever-new prez-era ever-hip as all that
ongoing junket in a jazz junk
ark that has gone
around and
around and
comes out
here

2008

## IN THE BOSTON MFA

There is no "African Art
In Motion Contexts".[5] What is a mask
without the masque? Dogon, Akan, Wolof
Bapende, Senufo, Maconde, Baga, Bambara:

what is a mask without drum
music, without the moving man or woman
within,
without the dance
without the prayer
or song??? Raised silence.

A still and quiet *bas relief,* a genteel museum
piece, hung just so, like "Strange Fruit."
Does dance hang on a wall?
Can prayer and song be shelved except in books?

But song needs silences to be musical.
Prayers need silence to be heard.
The word needs silhouetting silence.

Even so, artful Grand Acquisitors, Brahmin
grave robbers, shrine desecrators, by degrees,
took death masks
of copped cultures:

Inca copper, turquoise, jewelry,
Aztec gold and emerald jaguars
(they could not mine the sunshine, the light
or shadow of the undulating stone Mayan pyramidal
snake). Stone-tongues,
alabaster Babylonian tombstones, semi-
abstract African masks, attesting

to the manifests
of Manifest Destiny's slave-
ships, galleons and Conestoga wagons:
the fine art of genocide, after genocide, after...
What is a mask?

Across the deep
spiritual river renamed,
the Charles, after
spirited entreaties, recently returned English
ivy-covered Lakota
skulls warehoused at Harvard
returned to their context

*in earth and prayer,*
*in dance and dust,*
*in smoke and sky,*
*in the way the dead are meant*
*to come alive: masked*
*in motion and memory.*

1995

# ON JOHNNY CAKE HILL: A SONIC VISION

I leave the whale skeleton
in the museum on Johnny Cake Hill.

My own echoing footsteps
break the silence throbbing on
my ear drums.

Outside in the foggy day
the doleful foghorn's pulsing
wails roll up from the waterfront
regular as waves.  There is a break-
down by the curb of the quaint cobble
stoned street.

I assist a tourist, owner
of a fluke-tailed, white sedan
that is overheated, spouting steam,
parked on the other side

of the headlong road a whole nation's
taken to Profits Point. The owner
complains about his energy-eating car
but brags,

"It's got a smooth transmission.
Listen to…"
the mechanical melody,
a whale's song modulated,
the desperate sonar of an endangered
species.

The unseemly stream of sperm whale oil[6]
transmits a message. The whale's
sonic vision bounces off my ear drums.
I hear blues. The desperate sonar
of an endangered species floats up
from the bandstands and jukeboxes
of waterfront cafes.

A palpable truth rises from these
sea-green blues like ambergris,
like Queequeg's coffin.
As we push the car to the Whaling City Shell Station,

the whole world is held fast
to my ear, like a sea shell
in which I hear dying seas
and the extinction of singing things,
including us, in the cash register's

sounds, the mechanics of modulation.


1974

## KEEPING THE FAITH

We, the late legion American Africans
who fought
for Thee and Thy democracy,
for the dream to come
true, through thy revolutionary lie,
beginning with first blood, Boston's Massacre,
a cascading
spill which "...Tis of Thee...,"
begun for those who would try
to run us through, impale us, two
centuries later, on the Heritage Trail,
with our own eagle-pointed flagpole,

We hail and salute you![7]

We, too, the five score and more
thousands of late free colored,
bronzed in Common Park,
who fought in The Civil War to reaffirm
Liberty and Justice for all, who
learned we fought for Jim Crow, found freedom
was a dispirited Negro
spiritual, and sang
our red and white blues.
We, the cadenced, columned corps of colored soldiers,

We salute you!!

And those of us who chose and did not
choose to serve up our Negro limbs
our nerve and lives
in a segregated military service
during World War Two,
who back them wished for
a little more liberty to defend,

We salute you!!!

And we, the Blacks, the Bloods
who were through with you

by Vietnam, who
showed us which cheek you'd kick
if we turned the other, you
who in 'Nam would
call us *brother*, but not at home,

We salute you!!!!

And today? Today? Duty?
Booty?

Honor? Or oil? Country? Or Kuwait?
Saddam Hussein? The Fruit Plain?
Or Jesus' name? Today, come
what may, today we African Americans who are
about to die and don't know why

We salute you!!!!!


2003

## RED, WHITE, AND BLUES COUNTRY

In The Rainbow Grill
(a dark, white bar with a country box)
a rock salt and pepper corn

bearded, tri-colored Blood
in worn camouflage, torn
jeans, wearing broken, deep brown
shades, grimy baseball cap
and old, colorless cowboy boots,

played Cline's definitive rendition of "Crazy" over
and over. And spent all his green
for food stamps and rent
on sweet, warming, meriney wine,
chased by burning, fluid amber.
Bought the house many rounds…

Shots

leave him
cold, red-eyed
and blue, fingering the gold bands
and dog tags on the steel beaded chain

hanging from his…

…over and over. The record changes.
The old tone arm moves
from left to right;
he stands, stumbles
raises his glass as though to toast
someone, something.

Stares.
Muscles jerk.  Bent
over, he jukes
the joint, over and over, he hunches
heaving undigested supper,
lunch's sour mash, corned beef and cabbage,
breakfast's hash, fried egg

on toasted rye. He drops his empty glass.

Glassy stares like shards
in blood red faces
watch it and him "...*go*

*to pieces.*" Someone

says, "Greenie? He was
a four-tour Beret.
Hell, he'll be o.k."


1988

## UNDOING THE DO

Yes, as we have sung,
we *are* overcoming
and have come a long way
to get where we are
today.

But we are not beyond
The American Rite
of right-wing, night-riding
racism. Rightfully,

we rap, we brag on
how we are
survivors. Yes, we
have survived; some
few among us even flourish.

To survive
the horse-dragging,
car-dragging centuries'
social hells we had
to adapt to them
by the light of church

and cross burnings
in our souls. Adapting
to hells so well
some to some ex-
tent have emerged
from them some-

what hellish from the history,
by grand design. In mind
self-
generating slaves
salving festering sores
with the calming balm of THINGS.

So as we remember
Martin Luther King and

52

sing "We Shall Overcome,"
we need to free
our designedly
fractious, ununited selves

from escapist narcissism.
For ourselves we need
to ask why
we want,
we "need" to
live LARGE, instead

of "abundantly."

Why
we feel we need to
buy, to own, to drink,
to drive, to use,
to dye, or bleach, or fry,
or straighten

some of the things
we do. And why we do
some of the things
we do to and with our-
selves and one another.


1998

## KINDA BLUE: MILES DAVIS DIED TODAY

In print you told the world, the first imprint
on your ear's-eye was the tear-
shaped blue gas flame. Its organic funk
from things long dead. The burner's hiss

the sound of an afterlife.

Your indulgent, Garveyite father,
a dentist who didn't Shine grins,
spoiled you but saw that you grew black,
saw that you blew blueblack.
Taught you "America."
Taught you personal freedom, like love,
is a twelve bar blues, Dunbar's blue steel cage.
Showed you the way to play in
and the cost of playing out. In The City

caged, bar-bending Bird blew you away,
your mouth agape,
your wide eyes busted grace notes; slack-jawed,
you had no chops for Diz,
and you wallowed in wannabe.

You found your father's blues, found you
rang true, ROUND
MIDNIGHT, at the height of your humanity,
When The City's cop beat you for
being.
You
peeped the stacked deck of union I.D. cards
— for blacks only — pass books,
American apartheid, pointed
to the concert hall poster of your Horn-
Of-Africa face, modulated "My Nation
Tis Of Thee" to, This is me! This is me!!
The night stick played Langston Hughes' hard bop
on your head.
You bled blue notes
all over your white shirt, your vines
setting yet another trend:

54

blood-red blues.
Suited you to fit Bubber Miley's mute
to your belled horn, a plunger for the
burnt-out throat. Cool, ice blue artifice. You forged split notes
from metallurgy and alchemy of brass, shaped
the tear intense gas blue flame and burned.

*Burn Miles! Before the burner's turned off! Cook! You a gas!*

Your trumpet's voicing focused baby blue
spotlight on an inner intense tenderness, propane-flame-pure, spare
phrasings from the source of our spirituals
you gave birth to the cool.
Maybe too coolly, muting

rage in a silent way. Putting down
beating up what you love: you
woman-beating, Coltrane-smacking, Monk-abusing,
heart rending, not-so-funny valentine.
Beating up yourself, smacking your own
face with heroin, the near-death blow,
nearly out on Duke's "East St. Louis
Toodle O-O-O." Knocking yourself all the way down the dirty
dozen steps to heaven. Self-absorbed, yet
unselfish, generous with what really matters.

*You cool!! You bad!! You Miles!!! You "mother... ..."* you
dead but not IN A SILENT WAY.


1991

## DOT.DIS — A.I.

turned on
line the poet thought about
spell check on
the computer its lit up guard against ungainly syntax
lapses in sentence sense he remembered
the fabled chimp put in an imaginary room
with word processing on a laptop allowed hour glass
shaped eternity to randomly type on it at will would
reprint letter perfect at some point all of everything
previously written but the book of the dead everything under
our alphabet all transcribed oral literatures translated
holy writ rumi basho pessoa lorca invisible man
child in the promised land my bondage & my freedom he imag-
ined
things more timely than eternity in a quantum leap
of faith into the tempting garden in his own old apple two
what a piece of work
*damn*
inspired by the archetypal dollar green dull
lit screen he hunched he saw how some
time soon the ever evolving machine
if perfectly programmed for
subject slant world
view spin
such as humanist nationalist absurdist
for designated diction level mood mot
juste choices
for compositional aesthetics for lines en
jambed just so
for sound echoing nonsense for less is more or less
for sly syllabic rhythms pulsing patterns as easily
accessed as push button mode
modulations cash register changes on electronic music cross
over keyboards he was mindful that it was just
a matter of matter time space
before speaking computers would measure up
beat out feet mete
out verse more astutely than in
style neoformalist poets out
distance them by many meters by remote

amplification out perform stagey poets
volume wise
outtalk west winded erudite medieval guild gowned
poetasters' poeticisms on poesy &
the study of study
dons donned in classic
ally exclusive eurocentrism their doctoral bonnets
crowned with sonnets ahead
of packs & pods of the world's
moon baying deep blues sounding primal poets by degrees
these would be bedeviled how
like an angel by programming
*nmad*
infinite possibilities toward pat
personae he could see limitlessly
how it could be how
the computer printout could
would be original machine made universal poetry
a catchy trope trip on
an ananse the spider web
site the most innovative turn
off of
all time


2000

# ...TO YOU

*Dedicated to the late Jose A. Soler (1945-2020),*
*revolutionary labor activist, liberation educator,*
*fearless organizer, devoted father, grandfather,*
*comrade and much missed Brother In The Struggle*

*"First they came for the Socialists...I did not speak out...*
*and there was no one left to speak for me."*
*— Martin Niemoller (1892-1984)*

It always closes in on you the same way.

When it was about being
kidnapped (back) into slavery.

Or when peoples have been, are
plagued by epidemic genocides;

color-coded, race-and-gender or
faith-based oppressions such as

still raging pandemic patriarchies;
and when falsely accused, unjustly

arrested, convicted, wrongfully
sentenced just for being "other than",

having already been imprisoned
in poverty, or for slipping, falling

into the hole of addiction, home-
lessness; or otherwise scourged

as we all are presently by this
fast-spreading genderless, raceless,

classless, religionless, seemingly
apocalyptic covid-19 pathogen's

impending indiscriminate world-wide
wipe out of so many,


…Many Thousands Gone.


First it happens to a friend's friends' friends.
Then it's a few of your friend's friends.

After that it's an acquaintance.
Then a friend. Eventually, friends,

a family member or two.
Finally, in mind during daytime, in nightmare

during bits of fitful sleep you wonder
if what has happened and is happening

will happen…


2020

## TOGETHER: The Cheer

Alone so long
with longings

to get out, about, free
to safely be among massed

humanity. Individuals, couples
alone together,

families
together alone,

neighborhood, block,
house, apartment dwellers

separately together came
together separately.

On their respective
balconies, front porches,

front steps, stoops, sidewalks
more than safely distanced.

And exactly when their digital,
watches, clocks, e-devices screened

7:00 pm,
together

they clapped hands,
banged, clanged pans, pots

together, simply
shouted, yelled, cheered

together. Celebrated
their collective and individual

survival together. Unified in
live, happy, ritual clamor

together, cheering life-
saving nurses, doctors, life

itself together...
...Then in the somehow

singing silence, after
waves to, smiles at neighbors,

turned, walked or wheelchaired
back into themselves, into what

keeps them well, alive, social
distancing's isolation, separation

together. In the concentric contexts
of what ripples around self, love

of one another; the odd feel of even
distant family's presence, neighborly

separated but not estranged community;
within sight and hearing

of urban things that image or sound out
spring: climbing, twining vines, crab grass,

moss, pigeon, dandelion, sparrow, robin,
starling, finch through any window

to the natural world of which, yes,
the virus is a part. To "go" to church inside

the circle of themselves at the table, and pray
by saying grace in the words of any hopeful

utterance, by laughter with one another,
or by someone's anguished, angst-edged

outcry of *Why?* to whatever keeps us
together. Their quarantines' food boxes,

plastic storage containers' promises of something
lasting; fridge, oven openings; their peeling, paring,

cooking, eating, ongoing e-schooling,
remote working, e-playing, in-common-caring,

e-face-to-facings all act out the lived reply
to prayer remotely, singly and together.


2020

## ZOOM

has us
asking what

so many confessional poems
ask in their implicit ways:

*Can you hear me?*
*Do you see me?*

Every blued *i* needs
a platform, ID, connection.

Or harmonica,
guitar. Feel

me?

2021

# THE WEBB SPACE TELESCOPE

With this new way of seeing the universe,

back 13 billion years, dead galaxies
ghost light what was/is long gone: stars,

vast star systems which had lit colors human eyes
have never seen. By fired elements

not on our Periodic Table. We see the cosmic past
in the present, and what our Milky Way's future

will be. All at once. In one photo that looks like
a bottomless, transparent jar of brightly-colored,

lopsided jelly beans. All from a telescope picturing

what was from where there is no air, no atmosphere to blur
the *veritas* of its images. And nothing we see

is there anymore but is still ghost-lit by its recently arrived
light backdropped by the blackness of infinity, the nothingness

out of which everything came and comes (just as the late visual
artist Aldo Tambellini knew and painted). Including the binary star

system long since seen by the Dogon People of Mali, "Technicians
of The Sacred," who saw and see, knew and know -- without

a telescope -- Sirus B's 50 year elliptical orbit around Sirus A,
via time travel, not unlike Sun Ra's, on links of the interconnected

"web of existence of which we are a part."[8]


2022

# A POEM ABOUT EVERYTHING

> *"Everything is connected to everything else."*
> — *Leonardo da Vinci*

What is the difference
between difference & change,
change being the fundamental fact
of all existence? Ultimately,

there is only dark matter,
the so-called God
particle, gold-
colored

cloud-columns of cosmic dust, millions

of light years long, scoped through Hubble,
200 billion stars in our galaxy, at least
as many galaxies in our universe,

among parallel universes. Our own
domed domain? The "scientifically" or
religiously seen bubble of belief in which

we live? How

we "know" all that

yet never everything


about one another.  Everything is,

even all snow flakes are perfectly different

riffs on a theme beyond our ken, aspects of "is"

in infinite space where exact replications of everything


are not just likely but endlessly inevitable

among echoing silences between

throbbing radio waves of all


the algorithms of every species' heartbeat music


synthesized through bull rush reeded see-melody

saxophones such as those to which Sun Ra's life breath

gave voice on the other side of time, music being the other


side of being, where "poetry is another music"[9]

played on circular galaxies' spinning accretion discs

is more than a matter of matter. It is patterned

miracles, metered molecules amassed as

a visual music, Fibonnaci numbers[10]


are its random notes for The Way

of everything, the composition

of all of everything: the dark,
centered pad

of sunflowers, a nautilus' chambers,
pineapples, an elephant's trunk, our ears.
Does a molecule, amoeba, mite, mouse, man,
woman matter to the massive black holes that center

galaxies when there is no center to infinite space,
& all the matter that ever was, is, shall be
ever changed? What does it
matter when we who are down
from of the insighted outer-

spaced Dogon, Sun Ra's

ancestors, those who saw through time & space
to the fixed location of a binary star centuries
before telescoped arrogance of a science
more limited than religion could see it

through the dark matter of that science's
oppressive-isms, shades of meaning, spectrum
of belief when to so many not seeing was, is believing?

*We, The People,* who are the descendants of the Dogon,

decades before replying to our ritual, cultural greetings:

"What it is?" "Wussup?" "Wuss goin' down?"

with now hackneyed "It's all good." We


who made art out of our centuries of holocaust in Amerikkka. We

who rose on spirituals from rows of cotton, who gave indigo

hues to our red, white & black & blue blues & to all


this country's music. Whose?


We of the confluent culture that manifestly knows, shows

reality is as relative as a riff, who created the aural integers and

quantum mechanics of jazz, who know everything is interconnected,

who know life, all of creation is a big, smokin,' ever-ongoing

improvisation


an all-day-&-all night jam, every day, every night. We

the *all that* people, by way of greeting, meeting

with a smile, a hug and a shrug, as a matter

of the ethnic style that bent a dizzying[11]

trumpet toward "the angle of ascent,"[12]

that inclined us toward


"The President of The Saxophone's" hip slant[13]

as *down* and *on* as gravity, we simply said & some

of us in the USA say today in reply to "Hi, how are you?"

*Hey, everything is everything.* Why
not?


2022

# COMMUNION

## LOVE JAM

It was that rainy summer night
when Bobby Greene was playing
at the Pub.
He took out his horn,
did his *thang*,
and poured blue
milk into her ear.

She leaned near
and whispered to me.
It was the vaporous voice
of sax.

We picked up on the jam
and danced home
to do it to death:
a duet to life.

We sang all songs.
We danced all dances
until dawn came

up like song
on Sunday.

Dawn had a rainbow
wrapped around its waist,
and the pot
at the end of the rainbow
spilled over with

the alto rain of sax
and the baritone love-moan
of a saxophone.

1975

## COMMUNION

We embrace as history and future. We
walk along and up
but not away from the "Deep River"
our voices speak of.

She smiles all over
home where the blues are
never between the greens
and the cornbread.

*Let us break bread together*
*on our knees, on our knees.*
*Let us break bread together*
*on our knees.*

*Love as bread*
*cast upon the waters…*

Let us look away from obsidian mirrors.

After you sang so loudly in church,
how you do the dough.
Juju and Jesus root
through your hands. Roots.
Needin' the kneadin',

Sing the song Sister!!

Blood is in this cornbread,
corn in the bread, Baby,
sun in the corn, and a
son of Africa in the cornucopia eyes
lookin' this way is how you
rite a bread
with dough leavened with song,
baked hot with mandated melanin,
requisite to taste
this place's air.
There is a pestle and a gourd about
the act of kneadin' the tacky ova

74

of grain stained with sun.

Your cornbread.
The only blonde thing about you
gets down in the shiny bakin' pan
is a tambourine to glory
up into the oven as germ to womb…

Little bullied beans, black-eyed, punched out,
swell as siphons of the sauce

distilled from a swine whose funky soul
sacramentally
dances in the potted primal ooze and
around his own severed feet and side
steps as bacon drippin's in the chorus of
collards
on the amen corner of the stove,
holy rollin'
'cause cookin' is a kind of dance done
with the hands and heart.

Your stone-ground stirrin' countershakes
it, makes it fecund and arousin',
it is hotly kissed by fire
bakes it, and we
takes it.

Amen!

1973/1977

# NIA

At the beach
by the seeded ring cove,
she lay back, unbuttoned her
maternity blouse, knees funneled
moonsky and sea. Above
the sandbar there was a gold
ring around the moon. Stretch marks
rippled from her navel
cameo of time; tributaries flowed down around
her full-womb-stretched skin.

Moonlight unrolled
ancient scrolls of water
containing Middle
Passage names,
and her water broke
with Nia.

Nia, when they put you
bloody and immaculate
on your mother's elastic belly
skin, you kneaded your shadow;
love stared milk and your mother cooed

awe. Now

you cry for beamed moon juice
in this dark room.

Nia, Nia, Nia, Nia.
Herispapa'spoopoo;
*herishimfudgepudge*: Nia,
plump and healthy on your Mama's mana

smile, I pronounce your name.
*Purpose*, I pronounce your blood-red name
as your mother suckles you,
rocking in a bentwood chair built like
Bop, smiling crescent moons.


1978

# UMOJA

We put our infant daughter Nia
to sleep nestled, suckled, sated
three seats inside the hollow aisle
of the jumbo jet.

High over the Atlantic Ocean, flying through
the night with implicit faith in what is
flying us home through time zones over
human bones under the Middle Passage,
the deep dark outside the plane's star-scratched
windowpanes, holding hands all night to land,
at breaklight, at the place from where
all our dawns have come...

In the morning the jet's shadow comes at a coastal fishing
village like a shark. We step off the angled
plane onto ancestral soil to see
our footprints in the same deep red dust
our people have worked in Jersey, Georgia
and Jamaica.

At the sea-side resort,
we are served kola nuts and palm wine
in calabashes while hired hands play
kora and khalam and room keys exchange
hands and hands exchange soul shakes.

1978

## HOME TO GHANA

Home to Ghana to where
trees have leaves like green feathers
to where

birds have feathers like green leaves,
to where

dark brown women wear green
as beautifully as trees wear leaves,
to where

huge rock formations are
the hues, shapes of clouds,
to where

clouds have the hues, shapes
of rock formations and elephants,
to where

the red, iron-rich earth is fragrant
as baked bread after it rains,
to where

drums for sale, made from tree trunks,
hang by thongs from tree branches,
to where

circular, moveable, sculpted figures
of men are carved from one piece of wood,
to where

ebony stained, wooden *reliefs* of women
carrying Africa on their heads are sculpted,
to where
people fallible as anywhere
have the most perfectly shaped heads
of all humankind,
to where

there are black-coffee-colored

pre-schoolers so adorable in their

little white and indigo sailor suits,
that when God made them, God had to be
showing off!

1999/2014

# HOMECOMING

*The Pan African Writers' Association*
*World Poetry Festival,*
*University of Ghana, Legon*
*November, 1999*

*"Do ba-na co-ba, ge-ne-me, ge-ne-me!*
*Do ba-na co-ba, ge-ne-me, ge-ne-me!*[14]

we who are
american made who
feel and act like we are
making it in america

ensconced in mansions
with yachts
and other leisure craft
sometimes forget last

time we crossed

over the atlantic we
had to
we had

...we...

were so many too
few to...by twos
by the score in lots sold
singly or by the dirty dozens

baptized by inhumanity
in the name of the slaveship
in the name of our "owners"
and the power and the glory
of their successive sons many thousand-
thousands did not make it

...gone...

we who are american made

who act and feel like we
have it made in america some-

times forget

his craft and power are great
and still armed with steel gray greed
and hate that enforce foreign policy
begun with middle

passage forgive

the heavy air this plaint
brings to our affair
here you see
my great-grandparents' grandparents
came from somewhere in the old gold coast

indulge me you see the last time
the we in me crossed the sea
sickened naked branded we barely
made it we

traveled so lightly forgive
this funk those of us who
were not sick and jettisoned
like junk survived to make

possible succeeding amber waves of we
who currently seem to have it made
in america had seaborne ancestors
who in me are just recently airborne
here who
endured floggings and rapes in the name
of moral and cultural superiority who
bore up under ten stone bales of cotton
who rose in negro spirituals from christenings

in their own blood from baptismals awash
with their urine vomit liquid feces and pus
and walked free of the heavy air of the hold
into the sea-deep blues of american slavery

and its legacies pardon them
for returning in mixed company in me
for returning so ponderously my air
is heavy because I am here for them

fresh out of the funky hold of america
in the name of their lost forgotten family-
chain-linked names thrown overboard or other-
wise drowned in troubled water nameless
middle passage cape fear river "negroes"
gone
down drowned to be reborn
from kofi to cuffee to cousins
flourishing somewhere among the humanity

here i am

distant family extended nearly to the point
of no return but not as had been hoped for
by the slave breakers not beyond endurance
beyond belief for by-and-by real miracles

of rebellion escape cross-
overcoming by bullets ballots births
belief blessings
they are here in me
by invitation
by way of high john
hambone ring shouts jazz and pan
african airways

*"Do ba-na co-ba, ge-ne-me, ge-ne-me!*
*Ben-de, nu-li, nuli, nuli, ben-de-le"*

1999

## THE RETURN

We return with the ebony Seven Days
masks for which we haggled at the barracoon
beach boutique. Seven days carved as masks
we carry through time and customs. Beneath
the ebony stain they are grained like the life-

lines of our hands. A blue-eyed redhead at the
customs gate says,

Welcome home!

He checks all but the dju-dju bag hanging
by a thong from my neck. It holds: seeds,
black stone, red dust, root slice of a baobab,
a small sea shell from the east shore of the deep
hyphen between African

and American. We are returned to this
departure point without our shadows,
with what is
discovered with loss,
with what is
recovered with discovery.

1978

# WORD!

# BOB KAUFMAN?

No. I did not know him.
But here, in old New Bedford,
I hear New-York-based, Beignet-City-born,
baritone, redbone Bob Kaufman was a young
merchant seaman on the *The Ancient Mariner*.
In his twenties, in the forties, once or twice
on shore leave here he hung out all day drinking sky

blue moonshine from mason jars passed
around Afro-Luso to Afro-Anglo in befriending
*casas* or parked cars of Cape Verdean
American fellow National

Maritime Unionists. Or bought rounds
of barroom whiskey to oil their shared lunch
on lore and launched lies at the The Crystal Crioulo
Café where there were more "mornas" on the jukebox
than Storyville's Pops Armstrong or Kaufman's heyday
Lady Day. They say on shore he was a banned, standup labor

activist. At sea a damned good deckhand.
That on his off-
time he would bend
his lean frame over the bow, cast his net
of wishes, catch schooling
fish of fancy catch-as-catch-can.
Hauling in flitting, quick
silver sardines that glinted dripping sunlight, pull

up florescent daymares *de mer* from the melange bottom.
He would dry and smoke them and pack them
in his head. Called back and forth to California,
to The City by cyclonic causes
of the howling Manifesto Movement, he
left the ocean. Past parts of him are listed
on brittle browning manifests from a Middle
Passage vessel

and German Jewish migrant ship. Banished,
famished for his mother's homecooked, upright music

in their booklined living
room, he fed on free mumbo jumbo, Freud, Cesaire,
Fanon, Kafka, gumbo, goulash, and God
knows, man, whatever he could get panhandling.

Otherwise when empty stomached he drank in Bud
Powell's hip echoes of his homestead or toked
smoked dreams. Sometimes he retched our poetic
Rorschach's inkblot nightmare, his
life's work, piece by piece:

"What is America to me?"

Perhaps his light rum daemon,
his gin genie overly wrought their work on him,
but nonetheless, he wrote about the U.S.
in us with no "shit" and not a "motherfucker"
among his words. Perhaps he, like a lot of us,

mused too long in hard-lit barroom mirrors, saw
and felt us all in him and tried to drown
or numb the taunting lies and truths that stared
him down and out. But Kaufman's *in* again! Why?

Perhaps he was like Miles: self-
absorbed yet kinder to, more loving
of his art form, and, because of that,
more giving of good to all of us than him-
self or those in his life who loved him? He knew

back then any one of his poems
was more realized in our lives
than *The Declaration*.
He knew and wrote America was a *Murder
In The Cathedral*, a rape
in a museum school with moans among
the masks and bones and screams. Silence

he knew, too, was necessary if a jam was to be
heard over the din of institutional lies from
lecterns about: color, lack of color, "race," sex,
gender, power, money, *truth, justice, and The American Way.*

Though Bird-like in self-abuse, he was more
the austere, word-play Monk of poetry, sometimes
the sentimental, homespun Erroll Garner. But he was not
some sepia Breton, he was never
"the black Rimbaud." How

could he be? American
as red beans and rice, bagels and Buicks.
Hip as jazz. *Down*
as labor union dues and unemployment

blues. No, man, I did not know him.
But truths in some of Kaufman's poems
remind me, remake me better
understand myself, my context. And that
(aside from giving pure delight)
is one of the best things done

by any poetry or any person.
No. I never met him, but after
*The Ancient Rain* I hear and see
hungry Bob Kaufman
listening to Birdsong, knelled silence, songs about
black gardenias, and post-bop, post-Beat,
super-hip/
hop poets, listing to

port and vodka, spouting Eliot, scat-
ting, hopping onto the hood
of a gilled, fishtailed fifties car,
laughing and howling at the croissant moon.


2000

## WALKING KAUFMAN HOME

off and on
after your merchant marine
naïve quest for union
justice on land
at sea
after the full net of sun

glinting golden sardines
flying fish
american alchemy changed
to new coins with winged liberty
and dead anglo-american men on them (who

had freely charged their black label
bourbon and branch
sipped in the shade
of mythic history's
indian treaty tree

to slavery lynching
sweat shops' women workers
in mill town methodist factories) there

was the search for the sacred in saki
for divination in drug den
zen

after the twelve-bar blue
black solitary
bulb lit night with white

washed shadows of naked power
where the jail walls dripped mixed bloods
where bail was rarely made like fishes
and loaves
where time was kept
with nightsticks by cops
beating on the beatniks after bop's break-

light heavy brass-tinted bravura

response to war
after the long high
noon of stilled all-american moon

shine and vodka sipped in the shade
of a mountain-sized magic mushroom there
is still in silence

this inviting legacy:

wailed triumphs
raging cool
fires love
like Bird's bebop aubades
that fuse us that never refuse
our darkly lit humanness retelling the u.s.
in us all day after day after lady after-
life man you are still "ON"[15]


2000

## NAGASAKI

melted temple bells
tolling silences survive
memories flash points

2005

## PSALM '66

A psalm I sing of sixty-six!

Of sin I sing!
and science as God.
Oh, Lord, send down
LSD!
Mana sixty-six.

Eden again on the moon;
this time, will eve eat a rock?

The south I sing!
And soul of moses now in mississippi.
"Let my people go," yo!

A psalm I sing of sixty-six!

That God "is dead", it's often read,
but never computer proven.

The pill I sing!
That destiny's now digested,

I sing a psalm of sixty-six!

The psyche I sing!
the mind immortal,
conscience uncontested

and art unarrested;

the dance is in the discotheque
and drama's in "the toilet".

A psalm of sixty-six I sing!

Of sex I sing!
And that it's fully accepted,
more cave than allegory,
less catacomb than honeycomb,

more pleasure-dome than kubla khan,
more pleasing than pleasure.

I sing a psalm of sixty-six!

And, God, it's fun
this year and song!!
And even though the rice is red,
and even though the war is long,

a song I sing of sixty-six
and kicks,
a year of death and dance!


1966

## EVERETT/IMAMU/AMIRI

you could no longer be
just another beat
in the music

you booked from
an angry idyll
angst too
hip for words
& broke bad
you blued red
& white to
green black bloods…

…you remade yourself african as your own on
call for us to pick up hand carved fist
topped ebony lickin' sticks to drum
a steeled peace for our self

warring selves just up from
wholly stolen cargo people
shipped by the dirty dozens
to many thousand hellish places
via the good ship *zong* the *phillis* the *power*
& the *glory*
east to west

left of wright
the body of your work read red (will
never be a corpse &) always
plays the bridge be-

tween yesterday & tomorrow:
*to truly live you must*
*be your poetry*
*which should be is*
*your politics*
*your aesthetics*
*your ethic*
*your ethos world-*

*view too you*
*can't just*
*chant justice you struggle*
*don't just*
*say write unity you*

*need to must*
*be & do be*
*more than an imitation of*
*your imitators' shoo be doo be doo's*

& by the dozens hundreds
thousands tens of thousands
we by rite rewrote
our reality renamed ourselves named
our children kamal nia ayan reza
thought lived worked word
play clay africanized
the national hives' domesticated doo
be drone bees we became us
on our own heady raw black honey &
x'd old double crosses burned into our brains with cross-

pollinated poems
potent stinger pens
by any dreams necessary

out of your personal middle

passages you put down the pan pipe
cleared your hudson river reed of self
pith
freely tenored an old call
in another register
another key as we pitched
boxes full of forked tongue tea
leaves off the george washington bridge

you long since wrote all that was
word possible made worldwide earthtoned
connections your discordant choral chords
rearrange received histories'

choke hold languages' sour noted suite
of rum sung barracoon sea chanteys

at each reading you
return to us renewed
stand before us
blow red white black
& blue fact as gainsay
into the masked face of lone ranger racism
loudly read your "amerikkka" state

of the black art scat
"cherokee" from here
to "come Sunday" hum *home* by way
 of our elevated underground railroad
...*systems*...thru trane's "alabama" modulate "afrika"
to a brassy bravura based
 on the internationale
without one corny shoo be doo be doo


2002

# THE POET READ ALOUD THE COMPASS ROSE

*after jay wright
read his poetry at
the npf conference
1 july 00*

an archival red sea voice rose
from cordovan bound book pages
languages lined the round
horizon of saharan duned mind beyond
the thick-lipped obsidian olmec head

an afroandalusian sandman
stood before us
piped all hands on a bone fife

a day-dream

bowed a long love moan
out of a hairstrung cello
casal's heady wordless language

miles' canto hondo musings
about a muzzein's handcupped break-
light call to prayer
sweet as mothers
milk from an andean indian madonna's breasts

scored silence
in inner text
ancient as scrolled faith
hidden in the telling
shadowed holy
desert cave catacombs
of kings and desire

with solar
flare screams
of god-killed girls
who had
their stilled
bodies'

still beating
hearts hacked

out as offerings
to coiled priestly power
quetzalcoatl's feather
crested male authority

to bring in a good crop of sun-
colored mahiz long gone to el dorado
to dust yet ongoing in the singing of

        estevanico's[16]
        abubakari's[17]
        sea-loomed longings
        for loam

       *...i jee i naa*
        *i jee i naa*
        *i jee i naa*[18]

2000

## ...YOU

from
out of the ocean
islands geography

from
out of
geography history

from
out of history race-
based slavery and mixture

from
out of
mixture colonialism creolization

from
out of
creolization ancestry

from
out of
ancestry waves of *morna*-echoing ethos

from
out of
ethos community

from
out of
community *verde* hope

from
out of
hope love family

from
out of
family *mai pai*

from
out of
*mai* and *pai* brothers sisters

from
out of one brother more twinning
than twins'

from
out of
sororal love paula

from
out of
paula sisterhood more sisterly than sisters'

from
out of
the desiccated geography of necessity

the earth-toned facts of history
yesterday today tomorrow

from
out of
evergreen faith hope …


2015

## SUM OF ME: UN POKU DI TUDE

You ask me about me and my people? Me?
You can say as has been said and read in famous poetry:
"I am a part of all I have met." My people? Who
do you mean? Descendants of

The People who

were forcibly brought by sea from coastal Africa
to Cape Verde as slaves when the islands were green,
unknown, new to most of humankind?
Or from enslaving, colonizing Portugal,
of from Moorish Spain, Arabia, or Judea,
or all the world's ports-of-call?
Who?

*Maybe someone a lot like you?*
*They are all parts of me and I am part of them,*
*too.*

(Un Poku di Tude)

The People who

make my folk music, my sea-blue mornas,
my jazz, my gospel, my world music, and pop, too?
Singers, musician, music lovers of every hue?

*Maybe someone like you?*
*They are parts of me and I am a part of them,*
*too.*

(Un Poku di Tude)

The People who

keep on going no matter what, make do
and do without? Church-going
people who
"make a joyful noise unto the Lord" on Sundays
with a gospel shout and holler out "Amen!"?

*Maybe, my friend, someone like you.*

(Un Poku di Tude)

The People

who, like most, before they stand and sing
hymns to Him under their church steeple
Sunday mornings, just might like some loving
deep into Saturday night.

*Oh, yes, I am one of them and they are one in me,*
*too.*

(Un Poku di Tude)


2005

## NEO-GRIOT RAP

...What matters
is that our voices
are true to what was, is, can be
imagined, too. We have broken free of
imposed forms, from the outrages of being
bound in formal and informal cages. "Sympathy"'s
caged broken-winged song
birds now fly more freely that even
Bird's bop. They broke bad
with break-

dancing and hip

hop all over spoken word's poetry
perches
collectively-self-
liberated people's
poetry. Free
to be whatever

it wants to be,
what it is or is be-
coming. And what we have been
through entitles us to
tell it like it
tiz of thee.

What makes ours the poetry
of, by, for We The People
up from folk for whom it was
for far too long, in too many all-American
places —because of uptight "white rights" about
"races" — illegal to learn how to read
or write? We The People
descended from folk who
used to be the currency,
be the capital in capitalism's
centuries of "free market" slavery
and jim crow share-
cropping? History!

What makes my poem
a part of me, me a part of it?
A person out of a culture
with constantly copied and co-opted currency?
It's no mystery: ancestry, legacy,
class, politics, style. Confluence
of the mass mixed
things that come to mind
out of a "consciousness of kind,"
by way of belief, Civil War bullets,

Civil Rights ballots. Mixed-in out of
mouth things like gospel shouts,
signifying, jive, blues, jazz
songs, scat, the dozens,
r&b, break-
beats, rap. ALL that
black mouth evolved
north, east, west,
but first hybrid down
south of what
we used to say is
where it's at. Free

poetry, free
of the slave ship's choke hold,
free of the slave-breakers' silencing
iron bit. Freed
from verse cages of poesy.
Free to be what comes out
of its own history and its
current events, good as
they so often are and
should be. And bad
as they can so very
tragically be in
The Hood.

Liberated, up-
beat poetry. Be it
a penned declaration

of improvised oration as
an affirmation of its own, like
writing family, righting wrongs

riting home. Recite it, or write it,
or hear it, or read it like holy writ
because it is.
So be it.


2005

## SISTER SAY

Yo, Bro,
the other day,
I visited our local college campus
up the way. To hear what Sister Sonia Sanchez
had to say.

She's my favorite down upbeat poet of my generation,
one of the best & most relevant poets in our nation.
You read her out-of-sight, right-on rally poems, right?
The slamming one she done "…After The…March
For Disarmament"?

Anyway, let me tell you.
You oughta heard what Sister Sonia had to say
during her program's Q-&-A. Sister Sonia told us:
like it or not, we are all tied together by our tongues, knotted,
bound one to another by vocal chords.

Sister say, it's a new day,
say we need a better way to be
in this new century. Sister say, we need
a liberated, liberating language. One still real
enough to deal right when things are tough, things are tight.

But never a man-made dig or quip turned into a word-whip
(even in the name of what some think is hip),
Say, we need words
we do not use to rough up, batter, limit or otherwise
victimize one another.
No, not any human sister, human brother. Sister say,
always be about We,
The People, & free ourselves from mean words & deeds.

Sister say, let's rid ourselves of racist, sexist words. By rite
write hurtful words on recycled paper, cremate or bury them, let
them be
wiped out, in memory of all those African family names forcibly
drowned at sea
during our nation's free market slavery. Sister say, words
like "bitch" & "ho" have got to go. Say, so do those burned in

skin terms —

"octoroon," "quadroon," "mulatto," "negro," "nigger."
Sister say,
God knows, anyone is bigger than anyone of those.
Say, word-weapons, terms of abuse, don't get nicer behind
in-group-use.
That's no solution. Say, don't call anybody out of his or her
name. Say,
the rivers & our mouths are the same, & pollution poisons both.

So, Bro, in short, here's my report:
at that poetry program up the way the other day,
Sister Sonia say, there is no good bad
word. You heard?


2009

## SELF-HEXED REX AMERIKKKA: Post Katrina

*" . . . It is essential that we always repeat: 'we the people' . . ."*
— Sonia Sanchez, *"Poem for July 4, 1994"*

who put the hoodoo hex on you rex amerika?
you founding father of sally hemings' slave children you
who would drown all of us in the u.s. under
your man-made flood of bad blood you
who drowned many thousands gone in middle

passage . . . in cape fear river . . . in new orleans

you who drowned our ancestral african family
names in the holy water of those baptismals **We
The People** have a brassy bravura second-line to do
in your halliburton bottom-line you don't-give-a-damn
levee saboteur you *un*natural disaster of pox-infected

blankets tuskegee experiment "scientific" race-
isms benign neglect you who broke your own levee of lies
as you have all of your promises since *the declaration*
of your slavery-based "free" market nation **We**

**The People** have an upbeat dancing second-line
marching behind your mass murdering kind playing you
out of our minds escorting your dying self to the border of hell
while we knell you out with the red-white-&-black blues
tune "liberty" with your own cracked two-tongued bell **We**

**The People** with history's bloodknots who you
call have-nots who indeed have never had any homeland
security under you are heralding in a new order **We The People**
have always been playing you when we cake walked ragged

jazzed injustice high-five & slam
dunk our defiance of you from now to back when
you were an outright slave ship crew & right
up again to what we just went through in new orleans
which is hardly new behind your big easy behind

one of the capitols of capital (another being
the colonized mind) where you reign
over death for profit in the hood you who still steal
deal & otherwise sell souls having done it to us in the u.s.
since before we even got here the receded flood

of your bad blood reveals your graffiti-walled order
as the open book of devilish lies it wholly is you
commodifier of c.a.r.e. & compassion you
domestically violent white sheeted terrorist
you who profits from polluting the planet sabotaging

all of earth you who are intent on the mass
murder or incarceration of all of us in the nation who
do not abide by your will
be done
in

if you had your way but **We The People**
peeped that & say you had your day
rex amerika by
boomerang jet wings
by way of "bombs away!" over:

iraq
afghanistan
vieques
yugoslavia
sudan
panama
el salvador
libya
west philadelphia
grenada
guatemala
cambodia
vietnam
laos
peru
congo
cuba

you put a hex on yourself rex amerika
hey-day king of the may king of the *gras*
on a four hundred year old perennially new parade
float of bloated corpses
but **We The People** shall reign ourselves
when every day is may day **We The People**
a high-stepping brassy second-line shall be

behind you & do
& not for a closer walk
with your t'is of thee economy
rex amerika but to usher you
& your warring "business of amerika is business"
as usual at all costs youth-killer-kind out
to herald ourselves in

**We The People** seeking more than mythic white
dove holiday card peace & sunday morning love
of one another
an organized coalition of us in the u.s.
shall drown you out with gospel shout righteous rap
dialectics in diverse dialects more than token spoken

word protest anthems movement mantras with bible
& koran in hand in unity
& struggle to usher your deposed pimping
"show me something" ass out
rex amerika you founding
motherfucker
you


2005

# AN ELDER B.A.M. POET AT A BSU READING'S Q&A

*Baba Poet, what can a poem do about anything?*

Well, what did James Weldon Johnson's "Lift
every Voice and Sing" do for us back when
sometimes that sermonette-poem-turned-anthem,
and resolve, were all we had to collectively fuel
our faith and help lift, carry the burden of our
heavy hope

chest of goals, and to unite us in the
fight, move us forward? Our choral
singing of it was the moving, group aural
hug that inspirited The Struggle, made
us one no matter our number way
before "We Shall Overcome". And

what did "Dreams", "The Dream Keeper",
"I Dream A World", "Dream Deferred" by
Langston Hughes do for Dr. King,

for the most quoted American speech of the second
half of the past century and for civil rights? What
to do? Do what we have already done in ways

that have helped us get through it all.
Since 158 years before there was a U.S.A.
Do with words what we have done with
basketballs. Slam

dunk the truths about us in the U.S. the way
David Walker, Douglass, Ida Wells did,
n'do. Do with words what we have done
with dance.

Let your written poems' line-dance, on their pages, n'do.
Do with words what we have done with Double-Dutch as in Maya
Angelou's "Hopscotch", Jayne Cortez's

"Tappin'", n'do. Rally folk at righteous protest marches with-call-n-response rhythms. Do with words what we have done with jazz's voicings, as in Nina Simone's and Betty Carter's songs. Just as the Pharoah Sanders of poetry,
Askia Toure, does in his Kemetic epic, Dawn Song.
And, too, as Michael Harper does in Dear John, Dear Coltrane, n'do.

May your truth-carrying, witness-bearing words do us right, light your generation's way forward, out of yesterday, through today, toward tomorrow, n'do. So you, we,

remember the future the way your well-worded, testamentary predecessors', equity-and-justice-loving, politics-of-love-learned, revolutionary-love-loving June Jordan

and bell hooks did. Do your way what all-in revolutionary Amiri Baraka did for us with his unsheathed, razor tongue's weaponized truths' liberated, liberating way with language,

and inventive blues-Black takes on aspects of cultural tradition, n'do. So act on your insights and write, recite, righteously rap your rights. Rage

and organize, as if your, our lives depend upon it. Because they do! Note, as a teacher-poet-sage once wrote, "The first act of liberation is to destroy your own cage."


2023

# JAZZ THEOLOGY

# AS I EBB TOWARD THE END OF LIFE

*for Ryland, Chris, Kai, and Travis*

As a child at the shore
I was assured by my grown-ups
that if I held any sand-and-water-worn conch
shell to my ear, I would hear the sea,
even distantly.  And I did, or so it seemed to me.

And so in the summers of my prime

I assured the same thing to my own
water-borne children and held seashells
to their ears, asking them if they could hear
the ocean's roar and backdrop din
in the death-hollowed shells, and they would nod *Yes.*

Later in the mid-beach tide pools

of my consciousness on the east shore
of middle passage banked by bluffs of belief and sand
duned world history, I held hand-sized cowries to my ear
and heard sand-ground groaned prayers,
curses, cries, screams, pleas of several

centuries' many thousands-thousand gone
by slave ships into the bottomless blues
of the deep hyphen between African
and American.  But these post-prime days,

as time wears down my body

and the ebbing tide of life
weathers my mind,
just as succeeding waves of salty sea
water weather driftwood, at the shore,
watching my frolicking young grandsons play
in tide pools, and plash in the surf, and splash sea water
on one another, whenever I hold a spiral
remnant of a conch shell to my good ear,

I hear nothing but their healthy, joyful laughter.

2012

## imagine

not being

able to

remember who

you are,

or names,

and faces

of your

loved ones.

not being

even able

to remember,

*God*, how

to love,

to be

loving, and

who you

are, what

you are,

what you

did, not

do, where

you are,

where you

are going,

forget who

is gone,

what you

knew, imagined.

imagine forgetting

memorized poetry,

favorite songs,

how to

read, write

and talk,

or pray,

how to

compose poetry.

imagine your

body outliving your

mind. imagine

knowing all

that is

beginning. imagine

not being

able to

imagine.


2017

# IN THE KEY OF B

See, the nicest thing
that has happened to me
last spring to this one

was/is you

hugging me
from behind that night before
the Sunday service Mass
Poetry Fest gig
while I was improving
 on Hamlet's *to be or not*

*to be.* After my cancer therapy.

It was/is how you
had my back
by hugging me that way
that evening as I word-played
about my mortality.

You urged me
with a one-word coda
for all that had been said
and done, all that had been

neither said nor done,
you simultaneously, imperatively,
prayerfully, dead-
up lovingly said to me what still echoes
in my head:

*BE!*

It sounded like a voice from Above,
Around, Below, Behind, felt
like a warm kiss
on my spirit,
made me
feel

I

shall indeed continue through
my ailments and issues
to improvise me
in the key of b, G,

and be sharp.


2014

## SPIRIT

The ethereal entity
that sings itself in music;

can be seen in a kindness;
moves with, in

us during resistance against
injustice; embodies itself

in the felt way
of a hug.


2021

# INWARD MUSIC

*"We rarely hear the inward music,*
*but we are all dancing to it nevertheless."*
— *Rumi*

So there I was, this know-it-all but really half-hip kid who had
dropped out of college and created JAZZ, a deeper, yet more
*down*, more upbeat jazz zine than mainstream DOWNBEAT.
As editor I had scored this interview with the main big band man,
Count Basie. I had just caught both sets of the band's gig. A
guitarist myself, I had dug what could be heard of Basie's guitar
player, and I began my interview by presuming to hip Basie to
what I had heard as a bandstand weakness, aural flaw.

So after my expressions of awe and thanks, I asserted:
*I really like your acoustic guitar dude, but could just barely hear*
*him. And I was quite close to the bandstand, to the magic of the*
*music. So you know, I think it would be better if you put a mike*
*by the guitar player with him front and center, closer to us, the*
*audience.*

Still seated at the white baby grand piano, and looking annoyed,
Basie shook his head and said:
*No, my man, you don't understand. He doesn't play for you. He*
*plays for us. Freddie Green, our rhythm guitar man, is "The*
*Heartbeat Of The Band," rhythmically strings thing together for*
*us, you dig?*

Basie pushed up the shiny black visor of his bright white and
gold commodore's cap. Then began a brief riff on the melody of
one of his band's best known standard tunes, "Corner Pocket."
As he improvised on the piano I thought, On what strings
do my own doings swing? What/who guides my riffs on the
arrangements life plays out for me? How do I harmonize with
my own Higher Power on "Until I Met You?"

Basie stopped playing, looked over at me, nodded his head, said:
*Yeah, man, you can't hear him when he's playing, but you can*
*hear it when he's not!*[19]

2014

## JAZZ THEOLOGY

*"Jazz is my religion"* — *Ted Joans*

They had played everything from "C-Jam Blues" to "Come Sunday" but they were now playing their theme, and The Aristocratic Band Leader and Composer indicated with a nod that the time had come for the horn player to solo. The virtuoso slowly walked into the baby-blue spotlight, took a spread-legged stance, closed his eyes, and blew, made new what he had heard in the music…

…The Maestro cut him short. Why? His music moves in mysterious ways. The soloist lowered his ax from his mouth, opened his eyes and acknowledged the applause with a slight bow before he quietly walked back to his seat on the risers.

The Maestro winked at him, tugged on His gold, heart-shaped cuff link, rose from the piano, which was shaped like the continent of Africa, and swirlingly dance-conducted the starry host seated on the risers. He gave a nod to His next soloist, then stood on stage just above us, snapped His fingers to His Music's heartbeat swing dance rhythm while telling us in all tongues He loves us
*"…madly."*

1976/1992/2014

125

## AMIRI'S LAST SET:
## SYMPHONY HALL, NEWARK, NJ, JAN. 17, 2014

There was no more,no
more, no, yes, no more
musical poet. You
*who/who/who/who/who*
bopped up onto stages of
your life griot-

like, pounded podiums, turning them
into amplified congas nearly your size
with your dis-

proportionately large worker's
hands, as you connected the
sections of your poems by scat-

ting Monk, tuning the silences that
silhouetted the *RAZOR* sharp truths that
cut through the bullshit. Some thought it
was about lunch time by then (when all
had dished out their praise, whereas's,
wherefore's). But silently you reminded
us

it was really "Round Midnight," it was all there
on stage: hot black, brown, beige, yellow, white
stars with good chops giving you your props,

stage left of your silently echoing blues-like gallows
wit, wordlessly telling it like it t'is
of us in the u.s.

to We, The People

*who/who/who/who/who*
saw you there on stage to
the left of death in what
was/is

in fact the simple, evocative staged shrine,
you: a grained, brown, stand-up wooden stand
your height, topped with your jeff, your kente
cloth hanging

down from the wooden neck of it, looking
like age-and-work-bowed you —
*who/who/who/who/who* never bowed —
taking a final bow, bowing out and saying to
each of us in silent body language poetry,

*We'll be together again*
*at the protests, rallies,*
*organizing meetings,*
*polling places, voting*
*right by voting leftist.*
*Yeah, and we'll surely*
*meet again, my friend,*
*in THE MUSIC.*

2014

# Endnotes

1       "African Burial Ground" by Yusef Komunyakaa, *POETRY*, March 2014

2       Ogun is a Yoruba deity known as an Orisha, not quite a god, but a divine spirit. Ogun was worshipped as the divine spirit of weaponry, specifically metalwork.

3       As stated by then New Bedford mayor, Rodney French (1853-1854), a known abolitionist.

4       Shaw was a heroic sharecropper union organizer in early 20th century Alabama. *All God's Dangers,* his transcribed oral autobiography, won the National Book Award for its editor/transcriber, Theodore Rosengarten, without any royalties for Shaw at first.

5       *African Art in Motion: Icon and Art in the Collection of Katherine Coryton White*, by Robert Farris Thompson. Los Angeles: University of California Press, 1974.

6       Until relatively recently, some automatic transmission oils contained oil derived from sperm whales.

7       In Ancient Rome, gladiators, many of whom were from enslaved or subjugated peoples, would face the emperor or governor before a battle, salute, and say in Latin, "*We who are about to die, salute you!*"

8       One of the eight Unitarian Universalist principles

9       Sun Ra (1914 – 1993) –visionary, time-traveling jazz composer, instrumentalist, Sun Ra Arkestra band leader

10      A sequence of numbers in which each *number is equivalent to* the sum of the two preceding numbers, it dates back to ancient Sanskrit texts from 200 B.C.E., but was first brought to the attention of the Western world by Leonardo Fibbonaci.

11      Dizzy Gillespe, 1917-1993, American jazz pioneer, trumpet virtuoso, composer, educator, singer, and influencer/significant contributor to the development of jazz and bebop.

12      Robert Hayden, *Angle of Ascent: New and Selected Poems*, Liveright Publishing Corporation, 1975.

13      Lester Young, 1909-1959, jazz musician, was given the nickname "Pres" by Billie Holiday due to his unrivaled skill as the "president" of tenor saxophone.

14      From chapter 14, *The Souls of Black Folk,* by W.E.B. DuBois

15      "ON," Bob Kaufman (1925-1986), American Poet

16      Estavancio (1500-1539) was the Spanish-speaking African linguist and scout for the shipwrecked de Narvaez and de Vaca expeditions traveling from Florida to New Mexico and Arizona.

17      Abukari the Second of Mali was the transatlantic explorer who, some say, may have met pre-Columbian Mixtecs in 1310.

18      According to poet Jay Wright, this is an Ibo expression translating to "May you find your way home."

19      This is based on an anecdote shared with me by Tom Stites, writer and former *UUA WORLD* editor, originator of the title and spiritual practice presentations of "Jazz Theology."

# ABOUT THE AUTHOR

Everett Hoagland was born and raised in Philadelphia, Pennsylvania, but has lived in New Bedford since 1973 where he was that city's first Poet Laureate, 1994-1998. He was a full-time educator for four decades and is Professor Emeritus at the nearby University of Massachusetts Dartmouth in North Dartmouth, Massachusetts where during his 30-year career there he created and sustained four different African American literature classes in addition to his poetry writing workshops.

His poetry has been published in periodicals such as THE AMERICAN POETRY REVIEW, THE MASSACHUSETTS REVIEW, THE IOWA REVIEW, THE CRISIS, THE PROGRESSIVE, THE UUA WORLD, The CAPE COD REVIEW and has been excerpted in *The Boston Globe* and *Providence Journal*. Hoagland's work has also appeared in many anthologies since 1968, including *The Jazz Poetry Anthology, Bum Rush The Page, The Best American Poetry, African American Literature* (eds. Gilyard and Wardi), *The Oxford Anthology of African American Poetry, Afro Asia, Resisting Arrest, S.O.S., Ghost Fishing: An Eco-Justice Poetry Anthology, Liberation Poetry, What Saves Us* and *Black Fire — This Time*.

He received the Gwendolyn Brooks Award, two state-wide poetry competition awards for Massachusetts Artist Foundation Grants, two local Massachusetts Local Cultural Council Grants for book publications, The Langston Hughes Society Award, The Boston NAACP and Suffolk University Truth, Racial Healing and Transformation Initiative Award For A Lifetime Commitment To Black Liberation Through Art And Education, and The Stephen Henderson Award from The African American Literature and Culture Society. He is the recipient of the 2023 American Book Award For Poetry.

Hoagland's most recent books of poetry include *Ocean Voices* (third printing 2018), and his meditative collection *The Ways: Poems of Affirmation, Remembrance, Reflection and Wonder* (2022). He has given readings all over the USA, in Ghana, in Cuba and China. Much of his life's work and some memorabilia are archived in the W.E.B. Du Bois Library at the University of Massachusetts, Amherst.